Discovering The World Around Us

MEGALODON
The Biggest and Deadliest SHARK

TJ Rob

Megalodon

The Biggest and Deadliest SHARK

By TJ Rob

From the Discovering The World Around Us Series, Volume 3

ISBN 978-1-988695-09-9

Published by
TJ Rob
Suite 609
440-10816 Macleod Trail SE
Calgary, AB T2J 5N8 www.TJRob.com

TABLE OF CONTENTS   Page

What was a Megalodon?

Megalodons (Meg-ah-low-dons) were the biggest and most fearsome sharks that ever lived in our oceans.

Not only was Megalodon the largest prehistoric shark, but it was the largest marine predator in the history of the planet Earth.

The name Megalodon means "big tooth" in Ancient Greek.

5

When did Megalodons live?

Megalodons lived from about 25 million years ago until about 1.6 million years ago.

They became extinct about 1.6 million years ago.

With their immense size and strength Megalodons ruled the world's oceans for millions of years.

What do we know about them?

Like most sharks, Megalodons were cartilaginous fish. This means that their skeletons were not made of bone, but of cartilage.

A human's ears and nose are made of cartilage. Cartilage is a lot softer than bone and can bend.

If it is buried in the ground, cartilage does not last as long as bone.

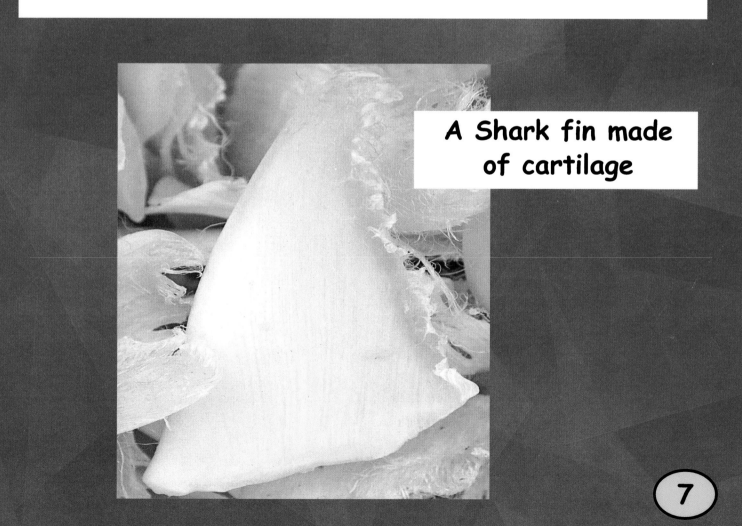

A Shark fin made of cartilage

The remains of any prehistoric creature that we find today are made of fossilized bones.

Because a Megalodon's skeleton was made of cartilage, we can find very little evidence of Megalodon at all.

A Fossilized
Megalodon Tooth

The only evidence that we find are the fossilized teeth and parts of the backbone or vertebrae of Megalodons.

Fossilized parts of the backbone or vertebrae.

What did they look like?

We are not sure what Megalodon looked like, because we have found so little of the remains of any Megalodons.

Because the teeth of the Great White Shark look similar to the fossilized teeth of Megalodons, Scientists believe that Megalodons looked similar to the Great White Sharks of today.

The big difference is that Megalodons would have been 3 times larger than the largest Great White.

Where did they live?

Scientists have been collecting fossilized Megalodon teeth from all parts of the world.

The yellow are the only areas where Megalodon *did not* live

Megalodon lived in nearly all the oceans

The only regions where no fossilized teeth have been found are in the far Northern regions of the Earth and the South Pole.

Megalodon preferred warmer water. At the time that Megalodon lived our oceans were warmer than they are today.

How big was Megalodon?

Scientists have been trying for years to decide how big Megalodons were when they were alive.

The best guess we have for the size of Megalodons is that they were somewhere between 50 to almost 70 feet (15.25 to 21.3 meters) long.

That is longer than a bus. The largest Great White Sharks today reach only 25 feet (7.6 meters) long.

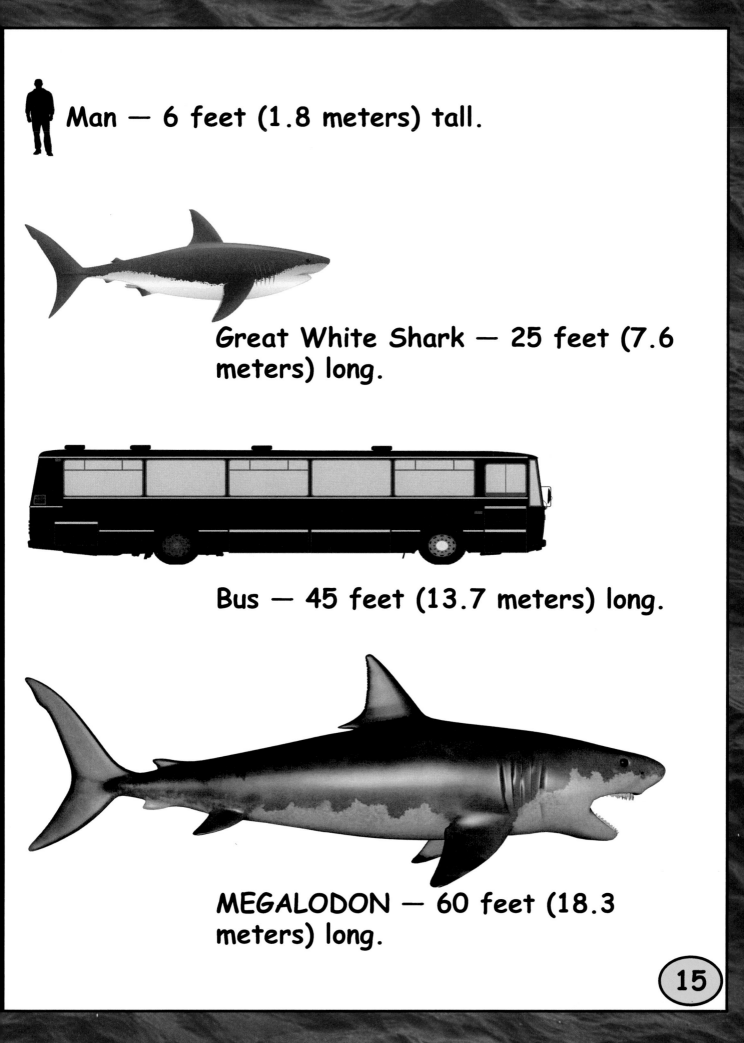

Man — 6 feet (1.8 meters) tall.

Great White Shark — 25 feet (7.6 meters) long.

Bus — 45 feet (13.7 meters) long.

MEGALODON — 60 feet (18.3 meters) long.

How much did a Megalodon weigh?

Megalodons weighed over 50 tons (100,000 pounds or 45350 kg) and some may have even reached close to 100 tons (200,000 pounds or 90700 kg).

Megalodon weighed more than 28 Great White Sharks!

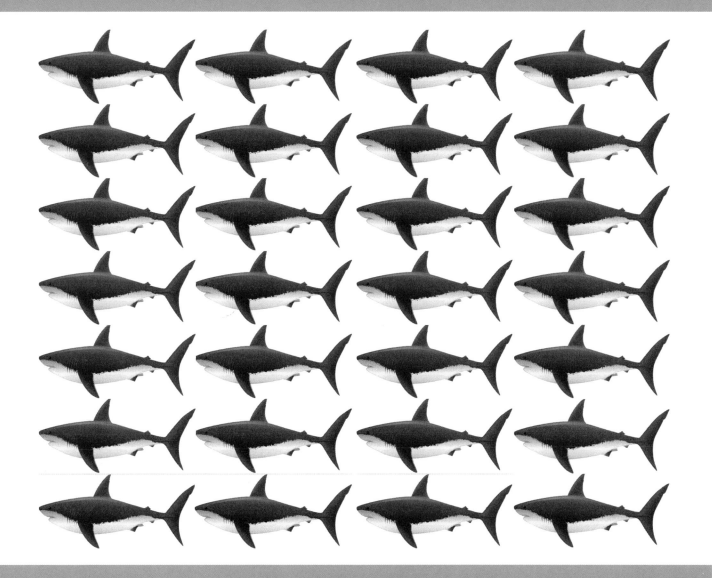

The biggest of today's Great White Sharks weigh only 3,5 tons (7,000 pounds or 3175 kg).

How big was the jaw of a Megalodon?
Twice the size of a great White Shark.

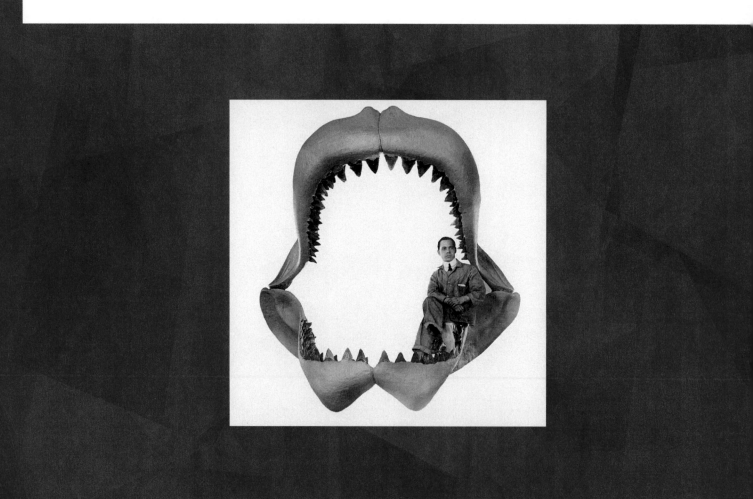

Scientists have calculated that a Megalodon had a jaw of between 8 to 10 feet (2.4 to 3 meters) across and 8 to 9 feet (2.4 to 2.75 meters) tall.

The tallest basketball players today could easily stand inside the jaw of a Megalodon.

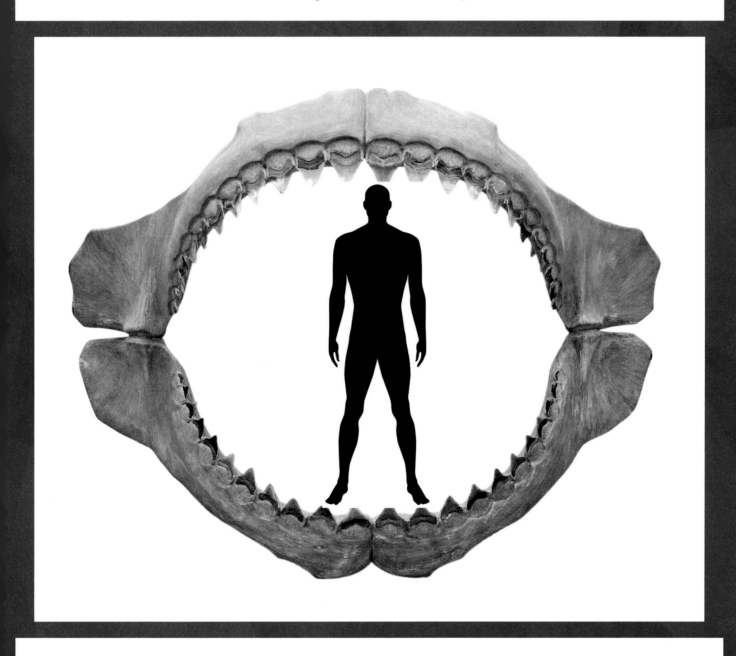

A Great White Shark today has a jaw that is only about 3 to 4 feet (1 to 1.2 meters) across.

Giant Teeth

Megalodon had huge teeth, nearly 3 times the size of a Great White Shark.

The largest Great White tooth ever found was less than 3 inches (7.6 centimeters) long, but the biggest Megalodon tooth ever found was almost 7 and a half inches (19 centimeters) long.

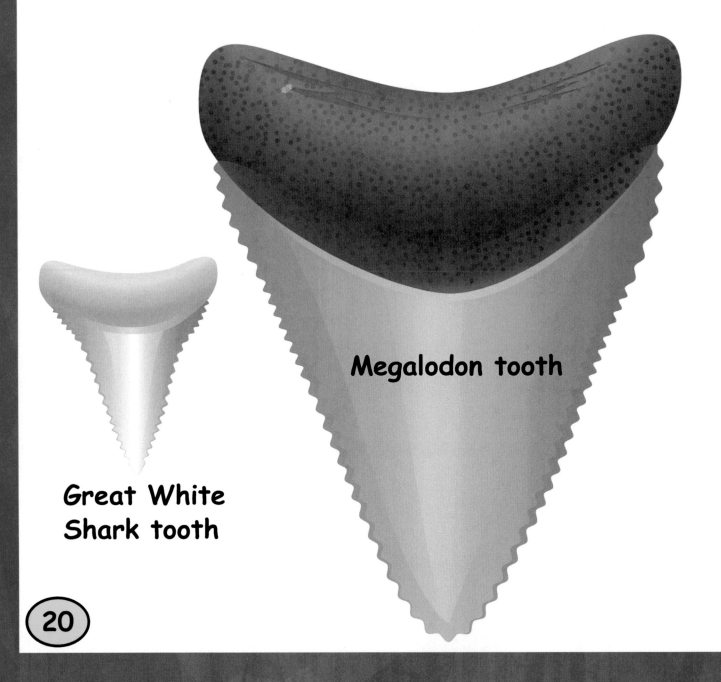

Megalodon tooth

Great White
Shark tooth

Serrated Teeth

Not only were Megalodon teeth huge, but they also had serrated edges, similar to a saw or a steak knife.

Serrated teeth cut flesh much easier.

How many teeth did Megalodon have?

Most sharks have at least six rows of teeth.

Megalodon had 46 front row teeth — 24 in the upper jaw and 22 in the lower jaw.

A Megalodon had about 276 teeth at any one time — if you added up all the teeth for all six rows.

Rows and rows of teeth in a Megalodon lower jaw

Did a Megalodon lose its teeth?

If Megalodons were like the sharks of today, they must have been able to replace broken and lost teeth throughout their entire lives.

A modern shark may replace its teeth as much as 20,000 times over the period of 25 years.

As one row of teeth begins to need replacing another row moves forward to fill in the missing teeth.

The teeth that are lost may float out to sea and become embedded in nearby rocks or sand.

Because they were always replacing their teeth, this may explain why we have found so many fossilized Megalodon teeth — more than any other part of the Megalodon's body.

Modern day
Great White
Shark showing
its teeth

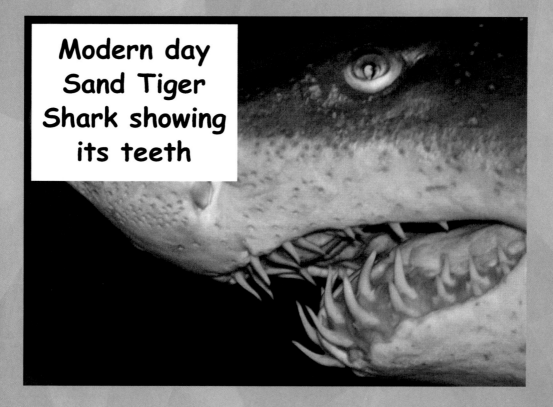

Modern day
Sand Tiger
Shark showing
its teeth

What did Megalodons eat?

Megalodons favorite food were marine mammals, but it also would eat other things.

Among the animals and fish it preferred to eat were dolphins, squids, whales (including very large ones like Sperm Whales), sea lions, porpoises and giant sea turtles.

Megalodon would use its powerful jaws to hunt its food.

It would clamp down and crush its victim's bones and the internal organs.

It also would use its teeth to bite off fins in order to immobilize its prey.

How much did a Megalodon eat?

A Megalodon could eat as much 2,500 pounds (1135 kg) every time it hunted for food.

No one knows how often it ate, but it must have eaten very regularly to keep its huge body alive.

Americans eat about 500 pounds (225 kg) of food in one year.

So in one single feeding a Megalodon could eat as much as one American could eat in 5 years.

What about baby Megalodons?

Even the newborn baby Megalodons were fairly large measuring between 6 – 11 feet (1.8 to 3.35 meters) long at birth according to scientists.

Megalodon was a warm water species that preferred subtropical climates.

While giving birth the warmer waters provided these sharks with lots of food sources.

How powerful was Megalodon's bite?

Megalodon had the most powerful bite of any creature on land and in the ocean that ever lived on Earth.

20 times more power in its bite than a Lion.

10 times more powerful than a Great White Shark.

7 times more power than even the T Rex (Tyrannosaurus Rex) Dinosaur.

The bite force of a Megalodon was calculated at 20 tons (40,000 pounds or 18140 kg).

This would be enough to crush a small car.

What was the lifespan of a Megalodon?

The estimated lifespan of the Megalodon was around 20 - 40 years.

A healthy and fit Megalodon may have lived even longer.

Scientists discovered pieces of Megalodon vertebrae or backbone, also called Centra. One piece of vertebra is a called a Centrum.

Megalodon showing where you would have found its backbone or centra made of cartilage

How do we calculate the age of a Megalodon?

Just like tree rings, a Megalodon would form a growth ring on each Centrum for every year that it lived.

A tree stump showing tree rings

Rings to be counted

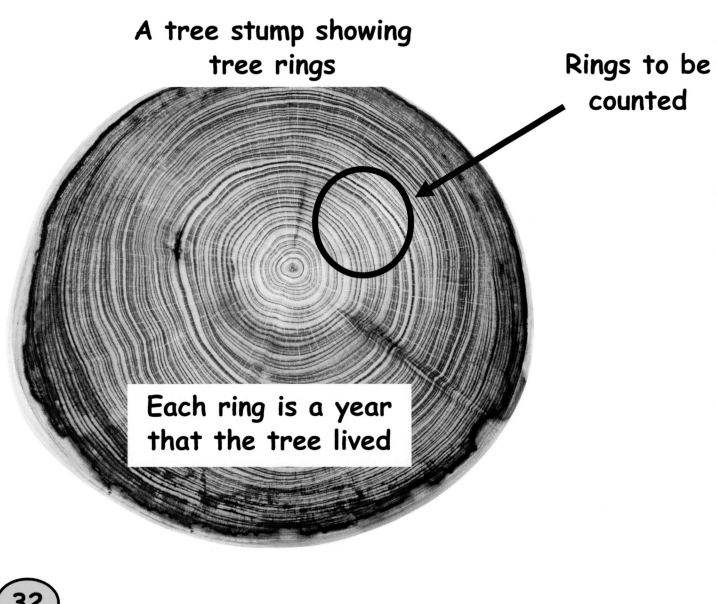

Each ring is a year that the tree lived

Pieces of the Centra help scientists to calculate the age of a Megalodon.

By counting the number of rings, we can get a very good idea of the age of the Megalodon when it died.

A Fossilized Megalodon Centrum (vertebra or backbone).

Rings to be counted

Each ring on the Centrum is a year the Megalodon lived

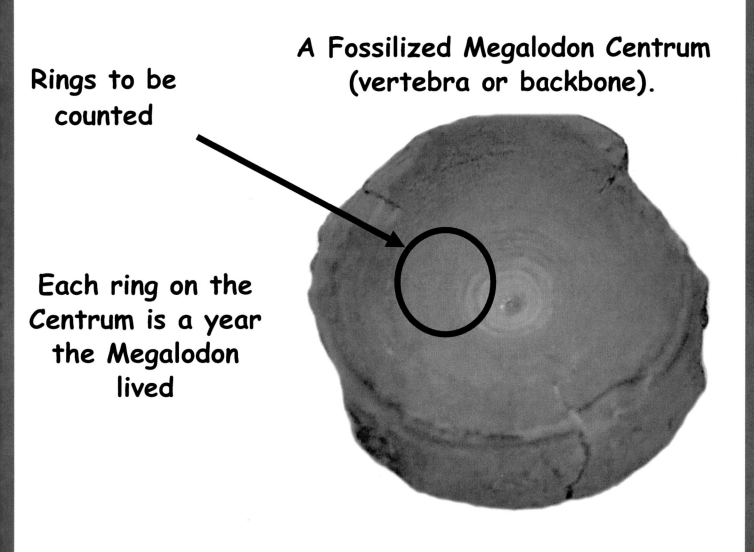

Why did Megalodons become extinct?

We may never know for sure exactly why Megalodon became extinct.

There may be more than one reason or explanation.

It is very likely that it is a combination of different events happening at the same time that caused Megalodon to die out about 1.6 million years ago.

Here is one possible explanation for Megalodon's extinction:

When Megalodon lived, the oceans were warmer than they are today. At the time Megalodon became extinct the oceans had become cooler.

Because Megalodon preferred warmer waters, and had such a huge body, it may have been difficult to cope with the temperature change. Cooler water meant less warm areas to live in with less prey to hunt and eat.

If Megalodon had difficulty in dealing with cooler oceans, other large animals may have had the same problems and started dying out too.

One of Megalodon's main food sources, an early type of Baleen Whale, also became extinct at the same time.

This meant Megalodon's food sources became more and more scarce.

Are there any Megalodons in the oceans today?

There is no evidence that Megalodons exist today.

With all the fishing and human activity on the ocean, no Megalodon has ever been caught or even seen today.

Could there be any Megalodons living in our oceans today?

No Megalodon teeth have been found that were younger than 1.6 million years old.

If Megalodons lost their teeth like we think they did, we would have found teeth belonging to present day Megalodons by now. So far none have been found.

Finally, with our ocean conditions being cooler, Megalodons would have difficulty living in the oceans today.

THANKS FOR READING!

Please leave a review at your favorite bookseller's website
- share with other readers what you liked about this book.

Visit www.TJRob.com for a FREE eBook and to discover TJ Rob's other exciting books

Made in the USA
Middletown, DE
21 August 2019